In appreciation
for who you are and
what you do

CCL Mentor Retreat

August 13, 2007

Because You Believed in Me

Because You Believed in Me

~

Mentors and Protégés
Who Shaped Our World

Marcia A. McMullen and Patricia M. Miller

**Andrews McMeel
Publishing**

Kansas City

02 03 04 05 06 FFG 10 9 8 7 6 5 4 3 2 1

Library of Congress Cataloging-in-Publication Data
McMullen, Marcia A.
    Because you believed in me : mentors and protégés who shaped
our world / Marcia A. McMullen and Patricia M. Miller.
        p. cm.
    Includes bibliographical references.
    ISBN 0-7407-2712-5
    1. Mentoring. I. Miller, Patricia M. II. Title.
BF637.C6 M383 2002
371.102—dc21

2002019798

Book design by Holly Camerlinck

For Helen

~

and the countless unnamed mentors
who open worlds for their protégés

Contents

Contents

Acknowledgments

Collaboration of any kind requires a common goal, a sharing of talents, and an enormous amount of support. Our understanding of giving has been redefined in the compilation of this work. We are beholden to several individuals who have made this process of creating meaningful:

The scholars whose previous studies and writings gave us the broadest scope for comprehending the intricacies of these great lives. Laurie Jacobi for her example of courageous persistence in bringing creativity to reality. Eminent research librarian Constance Carter at the Library of Congress and her assistant, Jennifer Harbster, who found in the rarest of materials the richest of information.

Our manuscript readers, Al Mauro Jr., Mary Kay McPhee, Jane Olsen, Susan Stanton, Bill Tammeus, Madeline and Ralph Wrobley, who understood our vision and made time to wrestle the manuscript, helping us to convey these rich stories with greater clarity.

Finally, to our families, who traveled the journey from conception to completion steadily, cheerfully, and lovingly, and at deadlines, carefully. They encouraged our effort to recount these stories from a unique perspective. They were our first *mentors*.

The voices of those who took time and gave their insights to me echo and abide with me. For their examples, I am thankful.

—PM

~

With gratitude to my mentor, Susan Stanton, for her faithful presence, edifying encouragement, and idea-shaping questions and conversations.

—MMc

Introduction

$\mathcal{I}$t is as familiar as the many word couplings used to describe this sometimes complex relationship: *master-apprentice, teacher-pupil, guide-novice.* Mentoring is ancient and ordinary, new and noble. Often without obligation, familial ties, or expectation, mentoring relationships are developed through mutual understanding and shared vision or values.

Mentoring requires openness, awareness, attentiveness, and time. Mentoring is elective and reciprocal. When the mentoring relationship is examined from the perspective of both mentor and protégé, it is clear that both benefit. Although this book is designed to inspire and uplift, another goal is to highlight the spirit of mutual generosity. The most important factors in the relationship are the protégé's receptivity and the mentor's enduring presence.

There were several influences that affected the lives of the protégés who are the subjects of this book. Each identified a mentor who served as a confidant, a guide, or a catalyst for his or her pursuits, or who introduced an idea or an opportunity. The mentor's steadfast participation affirmed the protégé's self-perception and occasionally his or her chosen course.

Some protégés indicated they were moved by the magnanimity of the mentor. Others suggested that it was the mentor's unyielding belief in their minds or their talents that encouraged them to continue through challenges. Several said it was the relentless nature of a demanding taskmaster that stretched them in ways never imagined.

Invitation was not necessarily part of the natural order of these relationships. Oftentimes mentoring occurred quite by happenstance. Sometimes these lives shared a similar interest, passion, or value, and that was where their worlds coincided.

Because You Believed in Me captures those elusive qualities and forms of mentoring relationships with historical examples. Through literary Polaroids, the timeless practice of mentoring is demonstrated by examining the relational understanding, emotion, and responsibility in the mentor-protégé relationship. The value of mentoring, tested by time, becomes apparent in the stories.

Measurement of results in social science confounds us. What difference does mentoring make? In an organized method or an informal encounter, can the worth of such a personal effort be specified? Can the outcomes of mentoring truly be known?

Historical examples provide results. These real lives help to prove theory. What if Eugène Boudin had not cajoled Claude Monet into the out-of-doors? Would someone else have inspired another person with similar talent to abandon an accepted practice of studio painting and venture into the beauty of landscapes? Joseph Haydn was able to see Wolfgang Amadeus Mozart's genius as well as assist in the cultivation of his talent.

People need an idealized sense of self, a hero. Even those who possess inherent brilliance or capacity need heroes, someone they can imagine they could be at their very best. The emulation of another can cause a discovery of one's self.

One of the outcomes of this research indicates that for many, success was not necessarily measured by the body of their individual works but rather by the process by which they achieved their distinction. Sharing their vulnerabilities and edified by the belief in another, they were moved beyond themselves.

Ultimately, the mentor's example, questions, and shared experiences helped protégés clarify their paths, crystallize their values, and experience the freedom to explore unimagined vistas.

In presenting these extraordinary individual lives and their impact on one another through committed acts of sharing wisdom and experience with others, we hope to inspire such generosity.

THOMAS JEFFERSON
Third President of the United States
1743–1826

~

GEORGE WYTHE
First American Law Professor
1726–1806

*V*iolinist, gardener, lover of music, architect, lawyer, and president of the United States, Thomas Jefferson cultivated numerous interests throughout his life with his deep love for knowledge. This long-nurtured discipline of learning was modeled in his formative years of study by his "beloved mentor," George Wythe.

After completing his two-year course of undergraduate study at the College of William and Mary in Virginia, Thomas

Jefferson began studying law under the tutelage of George Wythe, a dear friend of his undergraduate mathematics professor, Dr. William Small.

Preparation for a career in law in Colonial America primarily involved reading seminars, as the colonies offered no formal education in law. "Jefferson's years under Wythe, years of virtually uninterrupted reading, not only in law but also in ancient classics, English literature and general political philosophy, were not so much an apprenticeship for law as an apprenticeship for greatness."[1]

George Wythe was the first American law professor and distinctly the most reputable attorney in the colony of Virginia. Elected to the Virginia House of Burgesses and a member of Congress, later Wythe would also be a signer of the Declaration of Independence. He was a premier instructor who guided the reading and shaping of the mind and political philosophies of Thomas Jefferson. In his memoirs, Jefferson would call Wythe, "my ancient master, my earliest and best friend."

It wasn't simply Wythe's mind Jefferson found attractive but also his moral character, temperament, and commitment to fair and just methods of examining systems, issues, and people. Jefferson attempted to replicate the balance Wythe had achieved between the understanding of scholarship and his sensitivity in matters of the heart.

Theirs was a lifelong mentoring relationship punctuated by political issues, personal challenges, and a shared urgency to continue shaping America's freedoms.

Wythe was a quiet, practical man of well-chosen words and sentiments. He demonstrated his affection by unwavering devotion.

Jefferson frequently consulted Wythe on political matters. He sent drafts for review of what would become our Declaration of Independence, confiding in Wythe his anxiety around issues relating to judicial reform.

When Wythe died in 1806, he left the entirety of his library to his protégé. He felt that they might not be deserving of "a place in his museum, but estimated by my good will to him, the most valuable to him of anything which I have the power to bestow."[2] Giving to Jefferson the very books from which he learned his profession symbolized the fullness of their relationship.

Jefferson wrote fondly of his mentor, "No man left behind a character more venerated . . . This just and temperate man, devoted to human rights, was the honor of his own and a model for future times."[3]

Reverence knew no boundary in the map of this relationship. Decency, depth, and devotion characterized the Wythe-Jefferson relationship and their words live beyond them.

You, yourself, dearest friend,
during your last sojourn in this capital,
expressed to me your satisfaction with these works.

This, your approval, encourages me more than
anything else, and thus I entrust them to your care,
and hope that they are not wholly unworthy
of your favour.

~

Wolfgang Amadeus Mozart's dedication of six quartets
to Joseph Haydn

WOLFGANG AMADEUS MOZART
Austrian Classical Composer
1756–1791

~

JOSEPH HAYDN
Austrian Classical Composer
1732–1809

It is suspected that a 1783 Christmas concert in Vienna may have been where Wolfgang Amadeus Mozart and Joseph Haydn, two innovative classical composers, first came into each other's lives. Certainly, this is where the works of both men were performed. The program included both instrumental and vocal pieces by Mozart that introduced the intense passion between words and instruments. This passion quickly became Mozart's hallmark.

Mozart and Haydn became acquainted through shared talent and interest. Performing in similar salon circles with similar patrons, a mutual admiration emerged from their encounters. Haydn had full exposure to Mozart's budding talent, which revealed the younger man as a musical genius. While their personal interactions were infrequent, Haydn's profound effect on Mozart was immense.

Mozart began emulating the most distinguished characteristics of his mentor. For example, Haydn's masterful opera finales were exquisite in tone, tempo, and complexity. They came to be considered far superior to any composed by the Italians, who invented such stylistic grandeur. Less than a year after hearing Haydn's finales, Mozart adopted Haydn's structural style in composing *Figaro*. The composition surpassed the complexity of Haydn's creations.

Mozart certainly acknowledged Haydn as "teacher," though not in the formal sense. Mozart, as is true of many protégés, was motivated by encouragement from the mentor while ultimately desiring the mentor's respect.

Mozart repaid Haydn's meaningful attention with a public acknowledgment of his mentor's inspiration. After composing and dedicating six quartets to Haydn, Mozart wrote, "This, your approval, encourages me more than anything else. . . ."[1] H. C. Robbins Landon's biography of Mozart describes the dedication to Haydn as "one of the noblest of documents between friends."

Haydn found an opportunity to express his gratitude for

such distinction. On the evening Mozart first performed the quartets, Haydn said to Mozart's father, Leopold, "Before God and as an honest man, I tell you that your son is the greatest composer known to me either in person or by name. He has taste and what is more, the profound knowledge of composition."[2] This remark understandably moved Mozart's father to tears.

In December of 1790, Haydn went on to England and Mozart tearfully bid him good-bye. Mozart feared that would be the last time he would see his dear friend and mentor. It was. Just one year later, Mozart died.

Even after Mozart's death, Haydn continued to speak of his protégé's musical contribution: "Friends have flattered me that I have genius. But he [Mozart] surpassed me."[3]

Oh, this awful hush!

It seems impossible that voice is stilled
which I have loved to hear for fifty years.

~

Susan B. Anthony of Elizabeth Cady Stanton's death

SUSAN B. ANTHONY
Women's Rights Activist, Reformer, and Political Writer
1820–1906

~

ELIZABETH CADY STANTON
Leader of the Woman Suffrage Movement
1815–1902

*F*or more than fifty years, Susan B. Anthony and Elizabeth Cady Stanton together planted seeds of social reform, galvanized a nation, and nurtured a mentoring relationship. A common vision and great stamina allowed Anthony and Stanton to magnify issues of social injustice while enriching their lives and changing American history.

A street corner is where they actually met in the spring of 1851. Anthony and Stanton were introduced by a mutual friend on their way home from an antislavery meeting. Stanton recalled in her autobiography, "How well I remember the day! . . . There she stood with her good earnest face and genial smile. I liked her thoroughly."[1]

Almost immediately, Stanton recruited Anthony to join the movement of equality and justice for women. From that moment on, it would be "Mrs. Stanton" and Susan, sharing ideas, plotting reforms, and marshaling support for what was to become a revolution of ideas.

Elizabeth Cady Stanton, daughter of a judge, was from a privileged family in New York. As a young child, she came to understand why her father had so wished she had been a boy. Rights to own property, pursue an education, enter the professions, and vote were limited to men. Lessons from her father during her childhood of the dramatic inequality between the sexes formed the foundation for Elizabeth's future zeal for reform. Elizabeth mounted a campaign to bring about a change in the system.

A Quaker, Anthony was a single woman from Massachusetts with a passion ripe for activism. As a teacher, Anthony had felt the injustice of unequal wages. She earned one-fourth of the salary paid to male teachers.

Anthony joined Stanton at her home for weeks at a time preparing for rallies to promote the women's movement. During these long visits, Elizabeth would shape Susan's understanding and beliefs about feminism through many conversations and questions. This time helped to equip

Susan with the clear vision and tools necessary to carry the movement forward. Mrs. Stanton's guidance would not stop at the issues. She also advised Susan on presentation: "Dress loose, take a great deal of exercise, and be particular about your diet and sleep sound enough, the body has a great effect on the mind."[2]

These stays were by no means a friendly holiday or retreat; they were physically and intellectually demanding. Stanton and Anthony organized resources and cultivated expertise in the law. Elizabeth Cady Stanton had seven children. Susan alleviated some of Elizabeth's maternal and domestic chores. Sharing these responsibilities allowed the women to carve out a little more time to focus on the movement. Elizabeth's husband once remarked of their collaboration to his wife, "You stir Susan and Susan stirs the world."[3] An endless sharing of views blended their two worlds while deepening their commitment for reform.

"I forged the thunderbolts and she fired them."[4] Stanton said of her relationship with Anthony—a perfect match of mind, mission, and mutual respect. "In writing we did better work together than either could do alone. While she is slow and analytical in composition, I am rapid and synthetic. I am the better writer, she the better critic. She supplied the facts and statistics, I the philosophy and rhetoric, and together we have made arguments that have stood unshaken by the storms of thirty long years; arguments that no man has answered."[5]

"Anthony Left Behind," headlined a New York newspaper reporting the death of Elizabeth Cady Stanton in the autumn of 1902. These words factually demonstrated the culmination of their mentoring relationship and partnership, which the nation understood as unique. Separation of powerful symbols of a movement was cause for mourning.

Should my success be less than I desire,
and expect, the least I can say is,
the fault is not with you.

~

Ulysses S. Grant to Abraham Lincoln

ULYSSES S. GRANT
*U.S. General and Eighteenth President
of the United States
1822–1885*

~

ABRAHAM LINCOLN
*Sixteenth President of the United States
1809–1865*

What I want is generals who will fight battles and win victories. Grant has done this and I propose to stand by him. . . . Somehow I have always felt a leaning toward Grant. Ever since he sent that message to Buckner, 'No terms but unconditional surrender,' I have felt that he was the man that I could tie to, though I have never seen him."[1]

Abraham Lincoln, the sixteenth president of the United

States and the commander in chief of all the military forces of the Union, wrote the above comments after Ulysses S. Grant's victory over William Buckner's forces at Fort Donelson. It was the Union's first substantial victory in the War between the States.

Abraham Lincoln had tried and rejected six generals to lead the Union troops before he recognized the right man in U. S. Grant, the one who could succeed. Congress reestablished the rank of lieutenant general, previously held by George Washington. It was Lincoln's privilege to appoint a man to the position. After some delay, due to political jockeying prior to the 1864 presidential campaign, Lincoln named Grant to the rank.

"The new general-in-chief 'was the quietest little fellow you ever saw,' Lincoln told William Stoddard, one of his private secretaries. 'The only evidence you have that he's in any place is that he makes things git! Wherever he is, things move. Grant is the first general I've had! He's a general. I'll tell you what I mean. You know how it's been with all the rest. As soon as I put a man in command of the army he'd come to me with a plan of campaign and about as much say, 'Now I don't believe I can do it, but if you say so I'll try it on,' and so put the responsibility for success or failure on me. They all wanted to be the general. It isn't so with Grant. I'm glad to find a man who can go ahead without me. . . . He doesn't ask me to do impossibilities for him, and he's the first general I've had that didn't.'"[2]

In the short time from the Fort Donelson victory to the

spring of 1865, Lincoln and Grant's relationship grew primarily through correspondence. Analyzed in *Lincoln's Generals,* it was said, "In reality . . . Grant and Lincoln forged an effective partnership in a turmoil of clashing authority."[3]

The only extended period of time in one another's company was at City Point, Virginia, in March 1865. Grant invited Lincoln to visit the Union encampment, saying he would like to see Lincoln and that the rest would do him good.

Geoffrey Perret commented in *Ulysses S. Grant: Soldier and President*, "The rapport between the general in chief and the commander in chief was immediate and intense. They might as well have known each other from childhood. The bond was partly similar backgrounds, but it was more than that. 'Mediocrity knows nothing higher than itself,' observed Arthur Conan Doyle, 'but talent recognizes genius.' The spark of greatness flared in the presence of the other."[4]

"Amidst the confusion of war, Lincoln redefined the concept of commander in chief. . . . Charged with vast responsibilities, General in Chief Grant had to act vigorously within the military sphere, tread softly in the political sphere and understand as well the politics of command. Under Lincoln's guidance, sometimes oblique, sometimes imperious, Grant succeeded."[5]

A few days after his return from City Point, Abraham Lincoln was assassinated. "When he [Grant] tried to sum up the man [Lincoln], he could only say: 'He was incontestably the greatest man I've ever known!'"[6]

There is no time limit for mentoring; it is needed and can occur at almost any age. The lines can blur as leadership is asserted or acquiesced. Perhaps in this relationship, the faith and trust strengthened and grew in the two mature men complementarily. Grant and Lincoln needed each other, as the nation needed them.

The cordiality with which she welcomed me as a co-worker, I can never describe or forget. It aroused all my sunken hopes and energies and directed them again to the field of work which I had cultivated and which I had almost given up in despair.

~

—Marie Zakrzewska of Elizabeth Blackwell

MARIE ZAKRZEWSKA
American Physician
1829–1902

~

ELIZABETH BLACKWELL
American Physician and Medical Writer
1821–1910

$\mathcal{D}$r. Marie Zakrzewska trained in her native Germany as a midwife but was offered no opportunities to train as a physician. To practice medicine was her first desire. Marie immigrated to America to pursue her dream. After a series of initial disappointments in this new land, a friend made way for an introduction to Dr. Elizabeth Blackwell of New York, formerly of England.

Dr. Blackwell, as an established physician, knew personally

the challenge women confronted. The struggle to be accepted to medical school—ultimately Geneva Medical College (Hobart College) in Geneva, New York—was nearly equivalent to the narrow attitudes she faced once classes began. Blackwell became the first woman in the United States to graduate from medical school.

The first meeting was memorable for both women. Dr. Blackwell learned through their lengthy conversation not only of Marie's expansive knowledge and experience in midwifery but also of her impressive family history in medicine. Dr. Blackwell began to consider a way in which the two might work together.

Dr. Blackwell invited Marie to join her as an assistant in her newly opened dispensary, the New York Infirmary for Indigent Women and Children. Marie wrote in her memoirs, "I cannot comprehend how Dr. Blackwell could have taken such a deep interest in me as she manifested that morning, for I never in my life was so little myself." Marie continued, "She insisted that first of all I should learn English, and she offered to give me lessons twice a week and also to make efforts to enable me to enter a college to acquire the title of 'M.D.' which I had not the right to attach my name."[1] Cleveland Medical College (Western University) accepted Marie and awarded her the coveted M.D. degree in 1854.

Then the two women set to work on their next and mutual goal. They shared a similar desire to establish a teaching hospital and divided the responsibilities for bringing this to a reality. Marie was adept at raising funds to extend the infirmary while Elizabeth expanded the medical practice with assistance from her sister, Dr. Emily Blackwell. During the many stages in realizing their plans, Elizabeth and Marie would enjoy long walks discussing their vocation as physicians. These long talks allowed them to further conspire to help others, schemes that they considered pragmatic, restful, and hopeful. Dr. Blackwell wrote in her autobiography, "There is true stuff in her, I shall do my best to bring it out..."[2]

Shortly before Marie died, she acknowledged Elizabeth's influence in her autobiography: "Dr. Elizabeth Blackwell has been the most powerful agent in strengthening what was weak in me."[3]

I have not forgotten that it was first you who taught me to see and to understand what painting could be!

~

Claude Monet to Eugène Boudin

CLAUDE MONET
French Painter
1840–1926

~

EUGÈNE BOUDIN
French Painter
1824–1898

$\mathscr{T}$he paths of artists Claude Monet and Eugène Boudin crossed in a little frame shop owned by a Monsieur Gravier in Le Havre, France, where Monet and Boudin exhibited works. Monet, eighteen, displayed his caricatures, and thirty-one-year-old Boudin exhibited his landscapes. Gravier urged Monet as the young man looked over Boudin's seascapes to talk with the artist because of their shared interest in art. Boudin was someone Monet should meet. "Whatever people say about him, I can tell you, he knows his job. . . . He could give you good advice."[1]

Monet was reluctant to pursue such a meeting but one day happened into the shop when Boudin was present. The persistence of Monsieur Gravier led to what was to be an opportunity of a lifetime. After the two artists were introduced, Boudin remarked generously, "This young man has such a talent for caricature. They're amusing; they're full of zest, full of life." Turning to Monet, he observed, "You have a gift," adding, "I hope you're not going to confine yourself to this kind of thing. Study, learn to see and to paint, draw, and do landscapes."[2]

Boudin invited Monet to join him in painting *en plein air* ("in the open air"). The unique sincerity of this invitation prompted Monet to purchase his first paint box. Monet recalled, "Boudin set up his easel and went to work. I watched him with some apprehensions, I watched him more attentively, and then, it was as if a veil had been torn aside. . . . I had grasped what painting could be."[3]

For Monet, seeing Boudin paint allowed him to fully understand the intensity of the personal experience with nature, and it dramatically influenced his style. Plein air ideology was in direct opposition to the normal practice of artistry of the time. Studio artists relied on their memory of a subject, while the pleinairists experienced their subject first-hand. Monet suggested it was through this experience with Boudin that he was enabled to see a new world of possibilities. "Monet never sought to deny: 'If I became a painter, it is to Eugène Boudin that I owe the fact.'"[4]

A chance meeting of these two minds and the blending of their artistic experiences helped Monet cultivate his own distinctive style and exploration of subject composition. A simple invitation, an exposure to a worldview different from his own, presented a dramatic effect. Profound was Boudin's influence on Monet, but more striking was Monet's contribution to the history of art in the twentieth century.

When I first had the privilege of working under his personal inspiration he was already a physicist of the greatest renown, but nonetheless he was then, and always remained, open to listen to what a young man had on his mind.

~

Niels Bohr of Ernest Rutherford

NIELS BOHR
Danish Nuclear Physicist
1885–1962

~

ERNEST RUTHERFORD
British Nuclear Physicist
1871–1937

*A*t the turn of the century from nineteenth to twentieth, the time was right and ripe for physics—for harnessing the forces of nature and putting them to work for humanity. Observation, experimentation, and the formulation of principles about the natural world had been going on for aeons, a progression of understanding as one generation built on the insights of the last.

Practically and theoretically, the way was not smooth.

Ideas, instruments, data, and proofs had to accumulate and overcome obstacles such as ignorance and prejudice. However, within a brief half century, research and ideas, environment and people, would combine to ignite a revolution in scientific development—electricity, circuitry, relativity, atomic structure—the initiation of a new scientific age.

The ferment brought them together across national boundaries: students and teachers, experimentors and theorists. When Niels Bohr from Denmark, a postdoctoral student, first saw Ernest Rutherford from New Zealand, director of the Manchester Laboratory in Great Britain, they were in a crowd. This meeting at the Cavendish Laboratory in Cambridge exposed Bohr to stimulating people and valuable prospects in physics, his chosen field. A Bohr family friend introduced the young physics scholar and Rutherford, winner of the 1908 Nobel Prize in chemistry.

"Bohr's contacts with Rutherford set a stamp on the whole of his later scientific life…. [T]his influence stem[med] very little from what Rutherford taught him by way of physics. Rather, it was Rutherford's way of combining his own active research program with leadership in guiding younger physicists that made a lasting impression on Bohr and determined his own style from then on."[1] In a letter written during this time, Bohr related: "Rutherford comes regularly to hear how things are going. . . . [He] takes a real interest in the work of all the people working with him."[2] And later Bohr was to say, "To me he had almost been like a second father."[3] Rutherford's discovery of the nucleus of the atom led to the most important discovery by Bohr, the structure of the atom as a whole.

Inspiration flowed from Rutherford's "confidence and independent ways of making scientific judgements, his style of leadership, guiding others while vigorously continuing his own researches, and his concern for his younger collaborators."[4]

Looking back to the Manchester days in 1926 after he had also won a Nobel Prize (for physics in 1922), Niels Bohr remembered Rutherford's "confidence . . . Our admiration for his powerful personality was the basis for the inspiration felt by all in his laboratory, and made us all try our best to deserve the kind and untiring interest he took in the work of everyone. However modest the result might be, an approving word from him was the greatest encouragement for which any of us could wish."[5]

Throughout the remainder of Ernest Rutherford's life, he and Bohr sustained their professional contact and personal friendship. The development of the Institute for Theoretical Physics, built in Copenhagen, Denmark, during the postwar years, added to Niels Bohr's scientific and academic goals. Rutherford came from England before the construction was completed to deliver a lecture series in support of the institute. Later, when the facilities opened, Bohr, as the first director, wrote his first letter on the first day in his new office to Ernest Rutherford.

"From his earliest time in England, Bohr had looked forward

to international cooperation in the world of science. He was not thinking of atomic physics alone, but of a richer exchange between the various sciences and across national boundaries—not only for the sake of research, but also with the aim of paving the way for greater understanding."[6]

"When the great figures of the physics world met in Bologna to commemorate [Luigi] Galvani in October, 1937, Rutherford was already seriously ill and could not attend, and during the inaugural session the telegram was received. 'Rutherford is dead.' It arrived during Bohr's opening address, so that it fell to him, without preparation, to relay the news to the audience. It is said that he could hardly get the words out as the tears ran down his cheeks."[7]

Now went along these matchless early years
of master and apprentice.
Louis Sullivan, the Master,
and I, open-eyed, radical and critical,
but always willing apprentice.

~

Frank Lloyd Wright of Louis Sullivan

FRANK LLOYD WRIGHT
American Architect
1867–1959

~

LOUIS SULLIVAN
American Architect
1856–1924

$\mathcal{S}$ullivan needs help, Wright. It's difficult to find anyone to catch on to what he wants. I hope you succeed!"[1] With those words of Dankmar Adler, Frank Lloyd Wright joined the prestigious architectural firm of Adler and Sullivan in 1887.

The early years would be turbulent as he took his place in the firm as a draftsman. Wright's talent and pen work earned him the respect of Louis Sullivan, famed stylist and father of contemporary American architecture. Much to the chagrin of his coworkers, Wright was indisputably "the favorite." A section heading in his autobiography entitled "Combat" suggests he kept one eye peeled for fisticuffs and the other on his T-square.

"I became a good pencil in the Master's hand,"[2] Wright said about working for the aloof and demanding perfectionist. Each day gave way to a rich opportunity to learn and create. Sullivan relied on Wright for detail. Whenever he got the chance, he would blend the "sensuous efflorescence" of Sullivan's design with his own geometric lines. Then Sullivan would try to "bring me alive," as Wright recalled, "until I could make designs in his manner so well that towards the end of his life he would sometimes mistake my drawings for his."[3]

After seven prolific years of design, Wright secretly began moonlighting by designing houses. This abruptly ended his tenure at Adler and Sullivan and significantly distanced him from Sullivan.

The master–apprentice era would end for Sullivan and Wright, but Wright's profound respect for Sullivan's genius would endure. Wright integrated aspects of Sullivan's lessons of form and function and created his own noted Prairie style.

For both men, many practical disappointments would plague their lives: design disasters, lost loves, and reversals of financial fortune. They maintained connection through limited correspondence and, when needed, financial support.

Toward the end of Sullivan's life, Wright stepped in and made sure that Sullivan received proper care and had acceptable living arrangements. On Wright's frequent visits, Sullivan would share sample writings from his autobiography, *Autobiography of an Idea*.

On what was to be Wright's last visit, it was clear that Sullivan had markedly failed. Wright spent extra time with his mentor: "I was sitting by him, my arm around him to keep him warm and steady him. I could feel every vertebra in his backbone as I rubbed my hand up and down his spine to comfort him. And I could feel his heart pounding."[4]

Wright wrote some reflections on his mentor that were later published: "The New in the Old and the Old in the New is ever, Principle. Principle is all and the single reality my master Louis Sullivan ever loved. It gave to the man stature and gave to his work great significance."[5]

Sullivan's legacy to Wright embodied more than principle. Like a visible code of honor, the master's integrity passed to the one who "caught on" to his genius.

Carrel's mind flashed with the speed of light in space between the logical world of science and the mystical world of God.

~

Charles Lindbergh of Alexis Carrel

CHARLES LINDBERGH
American Aviator
1902–1974

~

ALEXIS CARREL
French Surgeon
1873–1944

*I*n 1938, Charles Lindbergh and Alexis Carrel coauthored *The Culture of Organs*. The text was the result of nearly a decade of experimentation and conversation prompted by family illness, probing questions about life and death, and each man's personal and professional capacities to take risks.

The partnership seemed unlikely. Lindbergh was a world-renowned aviator who flew alone from New York to Paris nonstop. He was a brilliant individual, a hero at twenty-nine. Dr. Carrel was a French surgeon whose innovation in vascular surgery brought him to the attention of the international medical community. In 1912, he was the first to be awarded the Nobel Prize in medicine.

Lindbergh's lifelong, intuitive interest in life's mysteries was rekindled by his sister-in-law's life-threatening illness, heart lesions. He had considered becoming a doctor like his two great-uncles, but he learned that a doctor had to be able to read and write Latin. Lindbergh's recollection was, "My first contact with high school Latin convinced me that the requirements for medicine lay beyond my intellectual desires and capacities."[1]

The search for medical help for his sister-in-law led Lindbergh to Dr. Carrel, whose practice and research at the time was in New York at the Rockefeller Institute for Medical Research. When they met there was an "instantaneous connection."[2] Dr. Carrel listened to all of Lindbergh's suggestions about how the proposed heart surgery could be performed and explained why some ideas wouldn't work. He also showed Lindbergh his experiments with a primitive perfusion pump.

Dr. Carrel offered Lindbergh the use of his laboratory for further experimentation on the mechanics necessary for successful organ surgery. Lindbergh spent time driving into the Rockefeller Institute from his home in New Jersey. Each idea and experiment was an opportunity to extend his conversations with Dr. Carrel.

Lindbergh would come to conclude at the end of his own life that Carrel had "the most stimulating mind I have known. . . . And so it was in the recalling the winter of 1930–31, Lindbergh began to balance in his mind an 'interest in aircraft with an interest in the bodies that flew them.'"[3]

Information and encouragement from Carrel and his wife assisted the Lindberghs in purchasing an island off the coast of Brittany, where they would live for two years with their second son, Jon. Having a home on Illiec freed the family from public scrutiny and allowed Charles to spend less rigorous times with his great friend and mentor, Alexis Carrel.

Carrel viewed Lindbergh as a hero and Lindbergh viewed Carrel as a hero. Their disciplines were different, but they shared a vibrant passion for life and a startling intellectual curiosity. Their minds met on extraordinary planes of new questions and ongoing pursuits.

He was a man and I was a boy,
and he gave direction to my life. . . .
What would have happened to me if I had
not known him in those eager and
impressionable years?

I would have had the same gifts, such as they are,
but would I have taken their possession
so seriously?

~

Alan Paton of Railton Dent

ALAN PATON
South African Writer
1903 –1988

~

RAILTON DENT
South African Educator
1898 –1972

*A*fter his first novel, *Cry, the Beloved Country,* was published in 1948, the world became acquainted with Alan Paton of South Africa. His literary talent was revealed in poetic descriptions of his country, dramatic insight into human behavior, and courageous social commentary. And although Paton would continue to write novels, poetry, biography, and his own two-volume autobiography, *Cry, the Beloved Country* gave him the financial freedom to increase his opposition to South Africa's apartheid policies and practices.

In biographies of Alan Paton and in his own autobiography, there are photographs that literally put faces to the life stories recounted. Parents and siblings, dressed neatly, look at the camera with somber, formal expressions. There are pictures of groups on holiday and in academic settings, fresh young faces—all white and all well groomed. As the years pass and Paton's career advances, the photos include the black and white faces of students in the schools where he taught. There is the Zulu school in Ixopo and the Diepkloof Reformatory, where he later was principal. A few images are of single individuals: wife, sons, and friends. These photographs, collected and chosen for their importance in Alan Paton's life, reveal the images of influence.

One particular face, a handsome smiling young man, is the image of Railton Dent, who, though six years older than Paton, began his first year at Natal University College at the same time as he. "This was not because he had been to war, but because he felt it his duty not to go to war. He was not a conscientious objector; he was a nongraduate teacher, and he intended to graduate and to devote his life to African education. He was the youthful principal of Edendale High School for African boys and girls, and he believed it was his duty to see the school through the war. Now that the war was over [1919] he felt free to take his degree."[1]

"The son of a Methodist missionary, Dent was a "committed Christian. Committed Christians have faults as commonly as other people, but [Paton] could see no fault in him."[2]

They became acquainted through the Students' Christian Association, which Railton—or Joe as his friends called him— invited Paton to join. Through this association, there was common interest, time, and opportunity to talk, listen, exchange ideas, ask questions, and build trust and respect for each other.

"It was Dent who first introduced [Paton] to Africans who were not servants or labourers, and that was to the teachers at Edendale school of which he had been the acting headmaster. And so [Alan Paton] met the first Africans who were introduced as equals. . . . It was not a giant step for mankind, but certainly a big step for [Paton]."[3]

The impact of Dent's friendship, as Paton assessed it in his autobiography, *Towards the Mountain,* many years later, was that Railton Dent became the greatest influence on his life by imparting one thing: "that life must be used in service of a cause greater than oneself."[4]

*I think my great love for my father
and the fact that he was so much interested
in photography was a strong added incentive
when I began work at the Clarence H. White School.*

~

Margaret Bourke-White of her father, Joseph White

MARGARET BOURKE-WHITE
American Photographer
1906–1971

∼

JOSEPH WHITE
American Inventor, Photographer, and Researcher
1870–1922

A Saturday-morning errand with her father to the steel foundry turned into a life-changing event as her eight-year-old eyes reveled in the glory of industry. "To me at that age, a foundry represented the beginning and end of all beauty. Later, when I became a photographer, with that instinctive desire that photographers have to show their world to others, this memory was so vivid and so alive that it shaped the whole course of my career."[1] New eyes, new perspectives, and new experiences would from that moment on be the driving force of Margaret Bourke-White's illustrious life, seeing beauty in the ordinary of industry and in the extraordinary of humanity.

Her father, Joseph White, introduced Margaret to images of mechanical intrigue. As an amateur photographer and inventor, he was a quiet but powerful influence on Margaret, offering daily opportunity for her to see a genius mind at work. Both inspired and befuddled, she watched the dedication her father demonstrated in his work and in his mind, never feeling that either was completely comprehensible. She recalled in her biography, a maxim her father both shared and modeled: "Never leave a job until you have done it to suit yourself and better than anyone else requires you to do it. Perhaps this unspoken creed was the most valuable inheritance that any child could receive from her father."[2]

Pioneering this fertile career of photojournalism happened as much by chance as it was by design. Her life and education would take a few turns before the course would be made clear for her world through the lens.

Margaret's father passed away as she turned seventeen. When she returned to school just after his death, she enrolled in a photography course with Clarence H. White. Later, as Vicki Goldberg's biography reveals, an interviewer wrote: "Her father is the chief reason for all Margaret Bourke-White has become."[3]

Inspired by the beauty of the Cornell University campus

in autumn and motivated by a need to earn money for school, Margaret Bourke-White began photographing the campus in its pristine beauty to sell as alma mater souvenirs to her fellow students. This successful business venture yielded much interest and quite a surprise when a student from the school of architecture inquired if this was a prelude to becoming an architectural photographer.

By Easter break, Margaret had hatched the idea of approaching an architectural firm in New York unannounced to get an objective opinion of her photographic work. At York and Sawyer, one of the architects, a Mr. Moskowitz, had an immediate interest and appreciation for her use of light and her eye for angle. It was enough to reignite the passion for revealing the dynamic force of light in the ordinary she had felt those many years before in the foundry with her father.

The 1920s brought hard work and much opportunity for the new graduate and tenacious photographer. She was granted entry into a world forbidden to women—the world of the steel mill. This assignment was unbelievably more difficult than she could possibly have imagined.

For one entire winter, keeping her day commitments, she went night after night to photograph the blast of the steel furnace. Many roles of film were discarded for various reasons: The tremble of the cranes would knock the camera out of focus, bursts of smoke from the furnace would appear on the lens, or there was not enough light to give definition to the lines of the machinery. Finally, with ingenious creativity, she used flares to illuminate the area. Of course, she had to convince two of her dear friends to hold the flares in their hands—first one, then two at a time.

This determined spirit and exemplary problem-solving skill would take her through the next decades of her career effortlessly—or so it seemed to others.

The editor in chief of *Time* magazine invited her to help with an innovative business magazine, *Fortune,* that would include photographs illustrating industry. Margaret eagerly responded, as she described in her autobiography: "This was the very role that I believed photography should play but on a wider stage than I could have imagined."[4]

Many aspects of her father's character and pursuits forever shaped her world: love for truth and the beauty of light, and his unyielding drive for perfection in his inventions. His example of dedication to his own creative genius encouraged Margaret to pursue her own talents and dreams and to expand her capacities without fear.

Startling images from the atrocities of war, the powerful machine of industry, and the quiet presence of Mahatma Gandhi at the spinning wheel have become the visual legacies of Margaret Bourke-White. Her photographs—which at times were social commentary—brought the age of industrial power to the nation's eyes and imagination, thus reflecting Joseph White's impact on her.

In my own case, I know . . . that when I began to read your poetry at college I think it immediately opened up my eyes to the possibility of the subject matter I could use and might never have thought of using if it hadn't been for you.—(I might not have written any poems at all, I suppose.)

Elizabeth Bishop to Marianne Moore

ELIZABETH BISHOP
American Poet
1911–1979

~

MARIANNE MOORE
American Poet
1887–1972

In "Efforts of Affection: A Memoir of Marianne Moore," Elizabeth Bishop recorded what she had observed and heard firsthand about her mentor. And, at the outset, Bishop commented about and gave credit for the memoir's title. "In the first edition of Marianne Moore's *Collected Poems* of 1951 there is a poem originally called 'Efforts and Affection.' In my copy of this book, Marianne crossed out the *and* and wrote *of* above it. I liked this change very much, and so I am giving the title 'Efforts of Affection' to the whole piece."[1]

Characteristic of their friendship and professional relationship through poetry—sharing, adapting, using words—the memoir/collected poems story is helpful for understanding them. With comparative study of both writers' works, it is possible to see or imagine similarities and preferences in the use of words and subject matter. It was, after all, their appreciation of and affinity for the English language that brought them together.

Elizabeth Bishop first met Marianne Moore in the spring of 1934, when Elizabeth was a senior at Vassar College, through Miss Fanny Borden, the college librarian. "I had already read every poem of Miss Moore's I could find. . . . I hadn't known poetry could be like that; I took to it immediately, but although I knew there was a volume of hers called *Observations,* it was not in the library and I had never seen it. . . . I finally got up my courage to ask Miss Borden why there was no copy of *Observations* by that wonderful poet Marianne Moore in the Vassar library. She looked ever so gently taken aback and inquired, 'Do you like Marianne Moore's poems?' I said I certainly did. Miss Borden then said calmly, 'I've known her since she was a little girl' and followed that with the question that was possibly to influence the whole course of my life: 'Would you like to meet her?' I was painfully—no, excruciatingly—shy . . . , but I immediately said, 'Yes.'"[2]

Returning to the original request, Miss Borden offered to

lend Elizabeth her personal copy of *Observations*. As she waited for the meeting in New York to be arranged, Elizabeth read the poems. They "struck her as miracles of language and construction. Why had no one written about things in this clear and dazzling way before?"[3]

The momentous event was arranged through Miss Borden. Miss Moore was willing to meet Miss Bishop at the New York Public Library on a bench at the right of the door leading to the reading room.

Elizabeth Bishop described their first encounter: "I was right on time, even a bit early, but she was there before me. I sat down and she began to talk. It seemed to me that Marianne talked to me steadily for the next thirty-five years, but of course that was nonsensical. I was living far from New York many of those years and saw her at long intervals. She must have been one of the world's greatest talkers: entertaining, enlightening, fascinating and memorable; her talk, like her poetry, was quite different from anyone else's in the world."[4]

While there is no record left by either woman of the content of their first conversation, "quite different from anyone else's" might have described Marianne Moore's reaction to Elizabeth Bishop's conversation as well. Each recognized and valued the originality of the other.

Moore encouraged Bishop to publish her poetry, contributed editorial suggestions, and recommended her for literary prizes. Bishop reciprocated by visiting the Brooklyn apartment where Moore lived with her mother, attending the circus and other New York events with Moore, and sending postcards and mementos from all of her travels—the things that friends do. And Bishop paid attention to the art and its craft that they held in common.

They were American poets, a generation apart in time. Theirs was a mentorship, "a story of artistic generations in evolution—Moore eccentric, generous, a willing critic; Bishop eager, feisty, grateful for Moore's friendship, yet working to chart an increasingly autonomous course."[5]

There was a bravery and a reticence in their first meeting superseded by the useful tension of differing ideas sharing a common passion for the written word.

Now I realize that my father's letters helped to form my mind in a way no other education did because they helped me to see things in perspective.

Indira Gandhi of Jawaharlal Nehru

INDIRA GANDHI
Third Prime Minister of India
1917–1984

~

JAWAHARLAL NEHRU
First Prime Minister of India
1889–1964

*I*ndira Nehru Gandhi was the third prime minister of India, the first woman elected as the chief government officer of a country that had won its independence from Great Britain. In 1947, her father, Jawaharlal Nehru, had become the first prime minister of independent India.

However, before there would be an independent India and before a Nehru dynasty of leadership could be imagined, the Nehru family lived in a palatial home in Allahabad, where the two great Indian rivers—the Ganges and the Yamuna—join. *Pandit,* meaning "scholar," was sometimes added to the family name and designated them as members of the highest Hindu caste. Inherited privileges distinguished them. Even the family home conveyed status and expectation by its name: Anand Bhavan, House of Happiness.

Momentum toward nationalism began to change the tranquillity and order of colonial India and Anand Bhavan by the year Indira was born. As Indira's father wrote to her many years later: "The great change came in our lives when you were a babe in arms. It is difficult for the younger generation to picture to themselves the world which vanished, it seems now, so long ago. . . . We have all become wayfarers and travellers marching on and on. . . . Yet, for those who can adapt themselves to this continuous journeying, there is no regret and they would not have it otherwise. A return to the dull uneventful past is unthinkable."[1]

At the House of Happiness, there were guests, meetings, and dinner-table conversations regarding the Indian National Congress, which had formed to promote communication between the Indian people and the British government and was to become a political party. These discussions brought the vocabulary and the emotions of the struggle home. The political and household turbulence affected Indira, the child.

"Like all children I suppose I asked a great many questions and, like all parents, my father chose which ones he should reply to. . . . Whenever he was at home he usually spent time talking to me. . . . Much of this was above my head: some things I retained and a lot I forgot."[2] What Indira remembered, she acted out seriously. Dividing her dolls into opposing groups of freedom fighters and baton-wielding police, she pretended the fight. In these imaginary battles, the freedom fighters always won. Gathering the household servants, Indira stood on a table and delivered political speeches to them. The Monkey Brigade, a group of children Indira organized, industriously and secretly put up posters, addressed envelopes, and carried messages to help the Indian National Congress Party.

Indira's formal education reflected the unsettled times as well; she attended several private schools in India and one in Switzerland. Often she was away from the House of Happiness, as was her father. Jawaharlal Nehru was deeply involved in political activities and often imprisoned because of them. "[H]er father felt compelled to make a contribution of his own to her education. In 1930, from Naini Prison, he started writing to her a series of letters which was soon to turn into a unique correspondence course in world history."[3] The first letter was written to Indira on her thirteenth birthday. "On your birthday you have been in the habit of receiving presents and good wishes. Good wishes you will still have in full measure, but what present can I send you from Naini Prison? My presents cannot be very material or solid. They can only be of the air and of the mind and spirit, such as a good fairy might have bestowed on you—things that even the high walls of prison cannot stop."[4]

These father-to-daughter letters, 196 in number, presented a world survey of history and a devotion that over three years of separation could only be expressed with pen and paper.

Circumstances continued to change for Indira, her father, and for India. By the time the goal of freedom had been achieved for their country, Jawaharlal Nehru was a widower and Indira was married with two sons. Father and daughter each had political and domestic responsibilities. The strength of their communication in honesty, trust, and care—as well as the demands of government affairs—drew them into a new phase of their relationship. Indira went to the prime minister's residence to help her father.

Far beyond the Monkey Brigade days of her childhood, but in the same spirit, Indira organized and managed the household. As her father's confidante and adviser, she accompanied him to Britain, China, the United States, Russia, and Indonesia—living and learning diplomacy at his side.

"Being my father's daughter it was inevitable that I should be fascinated by the uniqueness of India and her many-faceted personality and deeply committed (to the extent of merging my identity) to the welfare of her people."[5]

*Whatever you do, strive to do it so well
that no man living and no man dead
and no man yet to be born
could do it any better.*

Benjamin Elijah Mays to Martin Luther King Jr.

MARTIN LUTHER KING JR.
Baptist Minister and American Civil Rights Leader
1929–1968

~

BENJAMIN ELIJAH MAYS
Baptist Minister and American Educator
1894–1984

*H*ow did it begin, the relationship between the esteemed president of Morehouse College and the mesmerizing preacher of civil rights, the son of the rural South Carolina sharecropper and the son of the urban Baptist minister in Atlanta, Georgia, the Ph.D. from the University of Chicago and the Ph.D. from Boston University?

Awareness of each other would have been inescapable even in the large city of Atlanta. Martin Luther King Jr.'s parents and

Benjamin Elijah Mays and his wife, Sadie Gray Mays, who were married the same year Martin was born, were all members of the Baptist church, educated, and active in their spheres of the community. It was said that young King and Mays arrived at the Morehouse campus together: "King as a seventh grader at the Atlanta University Laboratory School, Mays as the President of Morehouse. Martin saw Mays fairly often that year, as it was his father's custom to attend concerts and lectures at Morehouse and Spelman [College] with all [of his] three children in tow."[1]

When Martin began his college education at age sixteen, he attended Morehouse. Each day on that campus began with a thirty-minute chapel service where Dr. Mays presided and spoke a message. "Martin fell under [his] spell. . . . This tall and erudite man, with his iron-gray hair and hypnotic voice, mesmerized his young disciples by preaching stewardship, responsibility and engagement.

"King was enormously impressed. He saw in Mays what he wanted a 'real minister to be'—a rational man whose sermons were both spiritually and intellectually stimulating, a moral man who was socially involved. Thanks largely to Mays, King realized that the ministry could be a respectable force for ideas, even for social protest."[2]

After his classes, King often visited Mays's office to discuss his studies and air his thoughts. It was Mays's turn to be impressed: "I perceived immediately that the boy was mature beyond his years; that he spoke as a man who should have had ten years' more experience than was possible. He had a balance and a maturity that were far beyond his years and a grasp of life and its problems that exceeded even that."[3]

The possibilities, the choices, and the dreams within King's student years were influenced by his family, his friends, his times, and the development of his capacities. When the call to ministry became clear to him, "he was more determined than ever to be like Benjamin Mays and serve God and humanity from his pulpit."[4]

Along the way, profound decisions were made: King's seminary studies at Crozer in Pennsylvania, postgraduate work in Boston, marriage to Coretta Scott, and then the question of where to begin his career. "As it turned out, several institutions offered him attractive posts—his old mentor and teacher, Benjamin Mays, tried to lure him back to Morehouse. But should he preach before going back to academe?"[5]

Martin accepted the pastorship offer from the Dexter Avenue Baptist Church in Montgomery, Alabama, in 1954, where, in the following year Rosa Parks would refuse to give up her bus seat to a white passenger.

At this watershed moment for the assertion of civil rights in America, Martin was called to leadership of the Montgomery Improvement Association. The emotions and convictions were strong. What would the Montgomery bus boycott and attendant issues and responsibilities demand of Martin? Speaking as an ally in understanding and support, Benjamin Mays made the prevailing point in a small council of family and friends: "Martin must do what he feels is right. No great leader runs away from the battle."[6]

However it began, it would end only with Martin's assassination in Memphis, Tennessee, fourteen years later. At Martin's funeral, after the service at Ebenezer Baptist Church (the church of his father), "the great cortège reached the tree-shaded campus of Morehouse College, where King had discovered Thoreau and found his calling under the guidance and inspiration of Benjamin Mays. Mays gave the eulogy, in which he said, "We assembled here from every section of this great nation and from other parts of the world to give thanks to God that He gave to America, at this moment in history, Martin Luther King Jr."[7]

*Just remember the world
is not a playground, but a schoolroom.*

Life is not a holiday, but an education.

*One eternal lesson for us all; to teach us
how better we should love.*

~

John Ed Patten to Barbara Jordan

BARBARA JORDAN
U.S. Congresswoman
1936–1996

~

JOHN ED PATTEN
Grandfather
1879–1958

*S*he was the baby girl. He was the grandfather of three little girls, but she was his favorite. On Sundays after church, Arlyne Patten Jordan, her husband, B. M. Jordan, and their daughters, Rosemary, Bennie, and Barbara, went to Grandfather and Grandmother Patten's house. Continuing a Sunday ritual—after sharing a meal prepared by Grandmother—the family dispersed to rest and later return to the church for organized activities and responsibilities. Barbara stayed at the

Pattens', first because she was too young for chorus or youth groups, later because she preferred to be in her grandfather's company.

The Patten home included a junkyard that was John Ed Patten's business. The salvage junk that he collected and sold surrounded him and Barbara. It was the scene of their life together. He taught Barbara to sort the junk into metal, papers, rags, and how to weigh and what to charge customers when they came. He always gave her part of the money. He talked and she learned. He listened and she grew. He trusted her to handle the money and hold on to it for him. In the evening after supper, John Ed and Barbara had time with the Bible.

The words were the same as other Bible words Barbara heard at church or in her parents' home. The explanations of the words were different. John Ed explained in a way Barbara could understand. Barbara said later in her life, "I understand Jesus and God better from my grandfather talking than from the church and that was because he communicated in a language I could understand. He was also saying that you couldn't trust the world out there. You couldn't trust them, so you had to figure things out for yourself. But you had to love humanity, even if you couldn't trust it. That's what he said the message of Jesus is."[1]

John Ed's Bible looked different, too. There were scraps of paper with red crayon writing tucked into it. These words he read to Barbara and referred to them as the gospel according to Saint John, meaning himself.

74

The love, acceptance, and material support such as he was able to give to his "black, smart, different, and special"[2] grand-daughter were wells from which she drew as life separated them. Through her years at Southern University in Texas, at law school in Massachusetts, in the state senate in Texas, and in the U.S. House of Representatives in Washington, D.C., Barbara was nourished by her grandfather's ways and words. On the day she died, at age fifty-nine, her pocketbook contained three unique items: a palm-sized copy of the Constitution and two photos of John Ed Patten.

Notes

Thomas Jefferson—George Wythe

1. Fawn M. Brodie, *Thomas Jefferson: An Intimate History* (New York: W. W. Norton and Company, 1974), 61.
2. Andrew Burstein, *The Inner Jefferson* (Charlottesville: University Press of Virginia, 1995), 134.
3. Ibid., 132–133.

Wolfgang Amadeus Mozart—Joseph Haydn

1. H. C. Robbins Landon, *Mozart the Golden Years, 1781–1791* (New York: Macmillan, 1989), 131.
2. Maynard Solomon, *Mozart: A Life* (New York: Harper-Collins, 1995), 314.
3. Wolfgang Hildesheimer, *Mozart* (New York: Farrar, Straus, and Giroux, 1982), 298.

Susan B. Anthony—Elizabeth Cady Stanton

1. Elizabeth Cady Stanton, *Eighty Years and More: Reminiscences, 1815–1897* (Boston: Northeastern University Press, 1994), 163.
2. Elizabeth Griffith, *In Her Own Right: The Life of Elizabeth Cady Stanton* (New York: Oxford University Press, 1984), 74.

3. Lynn Sherr, *Failure Is Impossible: Susan B. Anthony in Her Own Words* (New York: Time Books, 1996), 168.

4. Griffith, *In Her Own Right,* 74.

5. Stanton, *Eighty Years and More,* 166.

Ulysses S. Grant—Abraham Lincoln

1. Roy Meredith, *Mr. Lincoln's General: U. S. Grant: An Illustrated Autobiography* (New York: E. P. Dutton and Company, 1959), 20.

2. Brooks D. Simpson, *Ulysses S. Grant: Triumph over Adversity, 1822–1865* (New York: Houghton Mifflin Company, 2000), 273–274.

3. Gabor S. Boritt, ed., *Lincoln's Generals* (New York: Oxford University Press, 1994), 198.

4. Geoffrey Perret, *Ulysses S. Grant: Soldier and President* (New York: Random House, 1997), 349–350.

5. Bruce Catton, *Grant Takes Command* (New York: Little, Brown and Company, 1969), 479.

6. Ibid., 479.

Marie Zakrzewska—Elizabeth Blackwell

1. Agnes Vietor, *A Woman's Quest: The Life of Marie E. Zakrzewska* (New York: D. Appleton and Company, 1924), 108–109.

2. Ishbel Ross, *Child of Destiny: The Life Story of the First Woman Doctor* (New York: Harper and Brothers, 1949), 189.

3. Vietor, *A Woman's Quest,* 476.

Claude Monet—Eugène Boudin

1. Daniel Wildenstein, *Monet: Or the Triumph of Impressionism* (Paris: Taschen, 1999), 17.
2. Ibid., 18.
3. Ibid.
4. Ibid.

Niels Bohr—Ernest Rutherford

1. Abraham Pais, *Niels Bohr's Times: In Physics, Philosophy, and Polity* (New York: Oxford University Press, 1991), 16–17.
2. Ibid., 125.
3. Ibid., 129.
4. Ibid.
5. Ibid.
6. Niels Blaedel, *Harmony and Unity: The Life of Niels Bohr* (Madison, Wis.: Science Tech Publishers, 1988), 92.
7. Ibid., 272.

Frank Lloyd Wright—Louis Sullivan

1. Frank Lloyd Wright, *Frank Lloyd Wright: An Autobiography* (New York: Duell, Sloan and Pearce, 1943), 97.
2. Ibid., 104.
3. Ibid.
4. Ibid., 269.
5. Ibid.

Charles Lindbergh—Alexis Carrel

1. Scott A. Berg, *Lindbergh* (New York: G. P. Putnam's Sons, 1998), 223.
2. Ibid., 225.
3. Ibid.

Alan Paton—Railton Dent

1. Alan Paton, *Towards the Mountain* (New York: Charles Scribner's Sons, 1980), 58–59.
2. Ibid., 59.
3. Ibid., 63.
4. Ibid., 59.

Margaret Bourke-White—Joseph White

1. Margaret Bourke-White, *Portrait of Myself* (New York: Simon and Schuster, 1963), 18.
2. Vicki Goldberg, *Margaret Bourke-White* (NewYork: Harper and Row, 1986), 23.
3. Ibid., 23–24.
4. Bourke-White, *Portrait*, 64.

Elizabeth Bishop—Marianne Moore

1. Elizabeth Bishop, "Efforts of Affection: A Memoir of Marianne Moore," *Vanity Fair* 46, no. 4 (June 1983): 46–47.
2. Ibid.
3. Ibid.

4. Ibid.

5. David Kalstone, *Becoming a Poet: Elizabeth Bishop with Marianne Moore and Robert Lowell* (New York: Farrar, Straus, and Giroux, 1989), book jacket.

Indira Gandhi—Jawaharlal Nehru

1. Tariq Ali, *Indian Dynasty: The Story of the Nehru-Gandhi Family* (New York: G. P. Putnam's Sons, 1985), 147–148.

2. Indira Gandhi, *My Truth,* edited by Emmanuel Poughpadass (New York: Grove Press, 1982), 18.

3. Inder Malhotra, *Indira Gandhi: A Personal and Political Biography* (Boston: Northeastern University Press, 1989), 39–40.

4. Jawaharlal Nehru, *Glimpses of World History* (Asia Publishing House, 1962), 1–3.

5. *Indira Gandhi: Speeches and Writing* (New York, Evanston, San Francisco, and London: Harper and Row, 1975), foreword.

Martin Luther King Jr.—Benjamin Elijah Mays

1. Taylor Branch, *Parting the Waters: America in the King Years, 1954–1963* (New York: Simon and Schuster, 1988), 56.

2. Stephen B. Oates, *Let the Trumpet Sound: The Life of Martin Luther King, Jr.* (New York: New American Library, 1982), 18.

3. Ibid., 22.

4. Ibid., 23.
5. Ibid., 46.
6. Ibid., 90.
7. Ibid., 479.

Barbara Jordan—John Ed Patten

1. Barbara Jordan and Shelby Hearon, *Barbara Jordan: A Self-Portrait* (New York: Doubleday and Company, 1979), 9.
2. Mary Beth Rogers, *Barbara Jordan: An American Hero* (New York: Bantam Books, 1998), 25.

Bibliography

Thomas Jefferson—George Wythe

Bauer, Claude G. *The Young Jefferson*. Boston: Houghton Mifflin Company, 1945.

Brodie, Fawn M. *Thomas Jefferson: An Intimate History*. New York: W. W. Norton and Company, 1974.

Burstein, Andrew. *The Inner Jefferson*. Charlottesville: University Press of Virginia, 1995.

Dewey, Frank L. *Thomas Jefferson, Lawyer*. Charlottesville: University Press of Virginia, 1986.

Mayo, Bernard. *Jefferson Himself: The Personal Narrative of a Many-Sided American*. Boston: Houghton Mifflin Company, 1942.

Risjord, Norman K. *Thomas Jefferson*. Lanham, Md.: Rowman and Littlefield Publishers, 1994.

Sternz-Randall, Willard. *Thomas Jefferson: A Life*. New York: Henry Holt and Company, 1993.

Wolfgang Amadeus Mozart—Joseph Haydn

Hildesheimer, Wolfgang. *Mozart*. New York: Farrar, Straus, and Giroux, 1982.

Landon, H. C. Robbins. *Mozart: The Golden Years, 1781–1791*. New York: Macmillan, 1989.

Solomon, Maynard. *Mozart: A Life*. New York: Harper-Collins, 1995.

Susan B. Anthony—Elizabeth Cady Stanton

Anthony, Katherine. *Susan B. Anthony: Her Personal History and Her Era*. New York: Russell and Russell, 1975.

Barry, Kathleen. *Susan B. Anthony: A Biography of a Singular Feminist*. New York: New York University Press, 1998.

Dubois, Ellen Carol. *Elizabeth Cady Stanton–Susan B. Anthony: Correspondence, Writings, Speeches*. New York: Schocken Books, 1987.

Griffith, Elizabeth. *In Her Own Right: The Life of Elizabeth Cady Stanton*. New York: Oxford University Press, 1984.

Sherr, Lynn. *Failure Is Impossible: Susan B. Anthony in Her Own Words*. New York: Time Books, 1996.

Stanton, Elizabeth Cady. *Eighty Years and More: Reminiscences, 1815–1897*. Boston: Northeastern University Press, 1994.

Ulysses S. Grant—Abraham Lincoln

Abraham Lincoln: Speeches and Writings, 1959–1865. New York: The Library of America, 1989.

Boritta, Gabor S., ed. *Lincoln's Generals*. New York: Oxford University Press, 1994.

Catton, Bruce. *Grant Takes Command*. New York: Little, Brown and Company, 1969.

Chanwood, Godfrey Rathbone Benson. *Abraham Lincoln: A Biography*. New York: Madison Books, 1996.

Coolidge, Louis A. *Ulysses S. Grant*. New York: Houghton Mifflin Company, 1917.

Holland, J. G. *Holland's Life of Abraham Lincoln*. Lincoln: University of Nebraska Press, 1998.

Meredith, Roy. *Mr. Lincoln's General: U. S. Grant: An Illustrated Autobiography*. New York: E. P. Dutton and Company, 1959.

Perret, Geoffrey. *Ulysses S. Grant: Soldier and President*. New York: Random House, 1997.

Personal Memoirs of U. S. Grant. Edited with Notes and an Introduction by E. B. Long. New York: The World Publishing Company, 1952.

Simpson, Brooks D. *Ulysses S. Grant: Triumph over Adversity, 1822–1865*. New York: Houghton Mifflin Company, 2000.

Van Doren Stern, Philip. *The Life and Writings of Abraham Lincoln*. New York: The Modern Library, 1999.

Williams, T. Harry. *Lincoln and His General*. New York: Alfred A. Knopf, 1952.

Marie Zakrzewska—Elizabeth Blackwell

Lorber, Judith. *Women Physicians*. New York: Tavistock Publications, 1984.

Ross, Ishbel. *Child of Destiny: The Life Story of the First Woman Doctor*. New York: Harper and Brothers, 1949.

Vietor, Agnes. *A Woman's Quest: The Life of Marie E. Zakrzewska.* New York: D. Appleton and Company, 1924.

Zakrzewska, Marie Elizabeth. *A Practical Illustration of "Woman's Right to Labor."* Boston: John Wilson and Son, 1860.

Claude Monet—Eugène Boudin

Levine, Steven Z. *Monet, Narcissus, and Self-Reflection: The Modernist Myth of the Self.* Chicago: University of Chicago Press, 1994.

Rachman, Carla. *Monet.* London: Phaidon, 1997.

Schmit, Robert. *Eugène Boudin, 1824–1898.* New York: Hirschl and Adler Galleries, 1966.

Spatz, Virginia. *Claude Monet: Life and Work.* New York: Rizzoli International Publications, 1992.

Wildenstein, Daniel. *Monet: Or the Triumph of Impressionism.* Paris: Taschen,1999.

Niels Bohr—Ernest Rutherford

Blaedel, Niels. *Harmony and Unity: The Life of Niels Bohr.* Madison, Wis.: Science Tech Publishers, 1988.

Moore, Ruth. *Niels Bohr: The Man, His Science and the World They Changed.* New York: Alfred A. Knopf, 1956.

Niels Bohr and the Development of Physics. Edited with the assistance of L. Rosenfeld and V. Weisskopf. London: Pergamon Press, Ltd., 1955.

Pais, Abraham. *Niels Bohr's Times: In Physics, Philosophy, and Polity.* New York: Oxford University Press, 1991.

Robertson, Peter. *The Early Years: The Niels Bohr Institute, 1921–1930.* Copenhagen: Akademisk Forlag, 1979.

Rozental, S., ed. *Niels Bohr: His Life and Work as Seen by His Friends and Colleagues.* New York: John Wiley and Sons, 1967.

Frank Lloyd Wright—Louis Sullivan

Twombly, Robert. *Louis Sullivan: His Life and Work.* New York: Viking Penguin, 1986.

Twombly, Robert. *Louis Sullivan: The Function of Ornament.* New York: W. J. Norton and Company, 1986.

Wright, Frank Lloyd. *Frank Lloyd Wright: An Autobiography.* New York: Duell, Sloan and Pearce, 1943.

Charles Lindbergh—Alexis Carrel

Berg, Scott A. *Lindbergh.* New York: G. P. Putnam's Sons, 1998.

Lindbergh, Charles. *Charles A. Lindbergh: Autobiography of Values.* Harcourt Brace Jovanovich, 1976.

Alan Paton—Railton Dent

Alexander, Peter F. *Alan Paton: A Biography.* Oxford, New York: Oxford University Press, 1994.

Callahan, Edward. *Alan Paton.* rev. ed. Boston: Twayne Publishers,1982.

Paton, Alan. *Cry, the Beloved Country.* New York: Charles Scribner's Sons, 1948.

Paton, Alan. *Journey Continued: An Autobiography*. New York: Charles Scribner's Sons, 1988.

Paton, Alan. *Towards the Mountain*. New York: Charles Scribner's Sons, 1980.

Margaret Bourke-White—Joseph White

Bourke-White, Margaret. *Portrait of Myself*. New York: Simon and Schuster, 1963.

Callahan, Sean. *Margaret Bourke-White: Photographer*. New York: Little, Brown and Company, 1998.

Goldberg, Vicki. *Margaret Bourke-White*. New York: Harper and Row, 1986.

Silverman, Jonathan. *For the World to See: The Life of Margaret Bourke-White*. New York: The Viking Press, 1983.

Elizabeth Bishop—Marianne Moore

Bishop, Elizabeth. "Efforts of Affection: A Memoir of Marianne Moore." *Vanity Fair* 46, no. 4 (June1983): 46–47.

Kalstone, David. *Becoming a Poet: Elizabeth Bishop with Marianne Moore and Robert Lowell*. New York: Farrar, Straus, and Giroux, 1989.

Millier, Brett C. *Elizabeth Bishop: Life and the Memory of It*. Berkeley: University of California Press, 1993.

Molesworth, Charles. *Marianne Moore: A Literary Life*. New York: Antheneum, 1990.

Schwartz, Lloyd, and Sybill P. Ertess, eds. *Elizabeth Bishop and Her Art*. Ann Arbor: The University of Michigan Press, 1983.

Stevenson, Anne. *Elizabeth Bishop*. New York: Twayne Publishers, 1966.

Indira Gandhi—Jawaharal Nehru

Ali, Tariq. *Indian Dynasty: The Story of the Nehru-Gandhi Family*. New York: G. P. Putnam's Sons, 1985.

Gandhi, Indira. *My Truth*. Edited by Emmanuel Poughpadass. New York: Grove Press, 1982.

Gupte, Praney. *Mother India: A Political Biography*. New York: Charles Scribner's Sons, 1992.

Indira Gandhi: Speeches and Writing. New York, Evanston, San Francisco, and London: Harper and Row, 1975.

Jayakar, Pupal. *Indira Gandhi: An Intimate Biography*. New York: Pantheon Books, 1988.

Malhotra, Inder. *Indira Gandhi: A Personal and Political Biography*. Boston: Northeastern University Press, 1989.

Moraes, Frank. *Jawaharlal Nehru*. New York: The Macmillan Company, 1956.

Nehru, Jawaharlal. *Glimpses of World History*. Asia Publishing House, 1962.

Martin Luther King Jr.—Benjamin Elijah Mays

Branch, Taylor. *Parting the Waters: America in the King Years, 1954–1963*. New York: Simon and Schuster,1988.

Carter, Laurence Edward, Sr. *Walking Integrity*. Macon, Ga.: Mercer University Press, 1998.

Duffy, Bernard K., and Halford R. Ryan. *American Orators of the Twentieth Century: Critical Studies and Sources.* New York: Greenwood Press, 1987.

Garrow, David J. *Bearing the Cross: Martin Luther King, Jr. and the Southern Leadership Conference.* New York: Vintage Books, 1986.

King, Martin Luther, Jr. *Stride toward Freedom: The Montgomery Story.* San Francisco: Harper and Row, 1958.

Oates, Stephen B. *Let the Trumpet Sound: The Life of Martin Luther King, Jr.* New York: New American Library, 1982.

Walker, Martin. *America Reborn: A Twentieth Century Narrative in Twenty-Six Lives.* New York: Alfred A. Knopf, 2000.

Barbara Jordan—John Ed Patten

Hardy, Gayle J. *American Women Civil Rights Activists: Biobibliographies of Sixty-Eight Leaders, 1825–1992.* Jefferson, N.C.: McFarland and Company, 1993.

Jordan, Barbara, and Shelby Hearon. *Barbara Jordan: A Self-Portrait.* New York: Doubleday and Company, 1979.

Rogers, Mary Beth. *Barbara Jordan: An American Hero.* New York: Bantam Books, 1998.

Rothe, Anna. Edited by Evelyn Lohr. *Current Biography: Who's News and Why—1952.* New York: H. W. Wilson Company, 1952.

Whitman, Alden, ed. *American Reformers.* New York: H. W. Wilson Company, 1985.